Praise

Good Morning, Daughter is an outstanding daily devotional. With every enlightening and soothing entry, I felt the love and warmth of God speak to me and pull at my heart strings at just the right moments. We as humans and creations of GOD must realize that He is with us through both the good and the challenging times. This book reminded me of that. What a Mighty God We Serve!!! Great job!

Renee Rose

In *Good Morning, Daughter*, Angela Carter invites us into an adventure with the Father through a month of short yet profound daily meditations and scripture verses. These devotions inspire a sense of childlike wonder as "Daddy" speaks and shares His heart.

Mary Jo Rennert Gremling

Good Morning, Daughter

Good Morning, Daughter
31 DAYS WITH DADDY DEVOTIONAL

Angela Carter

© 2022 Angela R. Carter

All rights reserved. No part of this book may be reproduced, scanned, or distributed in any printed or electronic form without written permission from the author.

Scripture texts are taken from the King James Version unless otherwise noted, as follows:

ESV: The ESV® Bible (The Holy Bible, English Standard Version®). ESV® Text Edition: 2016. Copyright © 2001 by Crossway, a publishing ministry of Good News Publishers.

HCSB: Holman Christian Standard Bible®, copyright © 1999, 2000, 2002, 2003, 2009 by Holman Bible Publishers. Used by permission.

NASB 1995: New American Standard Bible®, Copyright © 1960, 1971, 1977, 1995 by The Lockman Foundation. All rights reserved.

NIV: The Holy Bible, New International Edition®, NIV® Copyright © 1973, 1978, 1984, 2011 by Biblica, Inc.® Used by permission. All rights reserved worldwide.

NLT: The Holy Bible, New Living Translation, copyright © 1996, 2004, 2015 by Tyndale House Foundation. Used by permission of Tyndale House Publishers, Inc., Carol Stream, Illinois 60188. All rights reserved.

RSV: Revised Standard Version of the Bible, copyright © 1946, 1952, and 1971 the Division of Christian Education of the National Council of the Churches of Christ in the United States of America. Used by permission. All rights reserved.

ISBN: 978-0-9899888-2-7

PRINTED IN THE UNITED STATES OF AMERICA
10 9 8 7 6 5 4 3 2 1

*I dedicate this book to my parents,
Sharon J. Brown and William T. Brown,
for showing what the love of God looks like.*

A Letter from the Author

Jesus has changed my life many times and in many ways over the years. This devotional God placed on my heart is a good example of that.

How did this book come to be? One evening after dinner with a couple of ladies, our conversation turned to life and Jesus. A woman turned to me and spoke prophetically: "You should sit with a pen in hand and allow the Holy Spirit to write through your hand."

Now personally, I hate writing, but the Holy Spirit is a whole different person. So, one day I began to quiet my mind and put pen to paper. This devotional is the result. It was created for you to have an adventure with Daddy.

I believe God is trying to show us how much he loves us if we just walk with him. That agape love is not like earthly love. It's eternal because the Father is eternal. My prayer is that this devotional will allow you to spend time with our Father, to help you grow and understand that your identity is in Christ the Father. May it bring you to a place of peace, joy, love, and adventure.

Love, your sister in Christ,
Angela

Good Morning, Daughter
Day 1

The sky's the limit today. We're walking out your salvation together. So don't think you're always doing things by yourself. I'm with you in the good times and bad times, cheering you on and stretching your faith. To believe the impossible, hold tight. I'm your Savior.

Enlarge the place of your tent;
stretch out the curtains of your dwellings, spare not;
lengthen your cords
and strengthen your pegs.

Isaiah 54:2 (NASB 1995)

Conversations with Daddy
Day 1

Good Morning, Daughter
Day 2

How excellent I am! The stars in the sky wink at me and you. You are my daughter, and all of the Earth responds to your voice because it responds to mine. You may not always see it, but it does, so choose your words wisely and follow me. I am the way. I am watching you grow as your faith gets stronger. Choose me, Daughter, choose me. I love you.

Life and death are in the power of the tongue, and those who love it will eat its fruit.

Proverbs 18:21 (HCSB)

Conversations with Daddy
Day 2

Good Morning, Daughter
Day 3

We are on a journey, you and I. It's a special journey full of many people. All the people are different. They all belong to me. I am the Father, and I know the plans. Some will follow my plans, and some will choose not to, but I am a good father, and they are my children. Stay on the journey with me, Daughter, and I will show you the way.

*"Which of you fathers, if your son asks for a fish,
will give him a snake instead?
Or if he asks for an egg, will give him a scorpion?"*

Luke 11:11-12 (NIV)

Conversations with Daddy
Day 3

Good Morning, Daughter
Day 4

How are you? I love you with an unfailing love. Do you see the clouds? They move in ways most people don't understand. That's how my love is for you. It's all around you. Beautiful and light. Able to get through any barriers you put up. See, Daughter, I am your creator, and I love you.

Neither height nor depth,
nor anything else in all creation,
will be able to separate us from the love of God
that is in Christ Jesus our Lord.

Romans 8:39 (NIV)

Conversations with Daddy
Day 4

Good Morning, Daughter
Day 5

Today is a special day filled with fun and clarity of mind. Walk upright, Daughter. See that you avoid the chaos and calamity, and don't let anything get in your way. I'm with you, holding you up and loving you until you leave this place and far beyond time. Tend to what I have given you, and I will always be there.

Love,
Daddy

*Even if my father and mother abandon me,
the Lord will hold me close.*

Psalm 27:10 (NLT)

Conversations with Daddy
Day 5

Good Morning, Daughter
Day 6

This is a beautiful morning. Thank you for sitting with me and spending time. I love you. You are my creation. I know you better than anyone in the world. You're my offspring, made in my image. The image of me. Look and live, Daughter. Look and live.

We are one and the same. Beautiful, beautiful and fierce. Keep your mind on me and you will stay in peace. I love you, and I will see you through this day. Don't worry or complain. This is a good day, ever so perfect in time. I love you.

Your Dad

So God created man in his own image, in the image of God created he him; male and female created he them.
And God blessed them, and God said unto them, Be fruitful, and multiply, and replenish the earth, and subdue it: and have dominion over the fish of the sea, and over the fowl of the air, and over every living thing that moveth upon the earth.

Genesis 1:27-28 (KJV)

Conversations with Daddy
Day 6

Good Morning, Daughter
Day 7

All is well. You know I love you, and you're my creation. Peace and grace abound in all my good works. Follow me and we will walk a journey worth walking, talking, and sharing. Understand why Daddy says what he says. You are my daughter. I love you, and you're special to me.

Love,
Daddy

For we are his workmanship, created in Christ Jesus for good works, which God prepared beforehand, that we should walk in them.

Ephesians 2:10 (ESV)

Conversations with Daddy
Day 7

Good Morning, Daughter
Day 8

What a great day this is. Rain is what feeds the Earth. My rain allows things to grow. You are in the rainy season, Daughter. I'm sitting with you. Keep focused. You will grow in this season. So don't worry, because worry is sin. I'm here, and you're my daughter, made in my image. I love you and I've got you.

After two days he will revive us;
on the third day he will restore us,
that we may live in his presence.
Let us acknowledge the Lord;
let us press on to acknowledge him.
As surely as the sun rises, he will appear;
he will come to us like the winter rains,
like the spring rains that water the earth.

Hosea 6:2-3 (NIV)

Conversations with Daddy
Day 8

Good Morning, Daughter
Day 9

How special you are to me. I love you. You're a beautiful flower in its most beautiful season. Full of color and light. My grace flushes over you, so special. I have plans for you, Daughter. Great plans. Follow me and know me. Move with me and grow.

*That ye might walk worthy of the Lord unto all pleasing,
being fruitful in every good work,
and increasing in the knowledge of God;
strengthened with all might, according to his glorious power,
unto all patience and longsuffering with joyfulness ...*

Colossians 1:10-11 (KJV)

Conversations with Daddy
Day 9

Good Morning, Daughter
Day 10

You are so lovely, and I love you. Don't be afraid of the days to come. I have everything under control, and we must go through these things. Listen, Daughter, listen and you will find me speaking and giving you wisdom on the journey. Spend time with me. Be still. I have everything under control.

Love,
Daddy

The plans of the diligent lead to profit
as surely as haste leads to poverty.

Proverbs 21:5 (NIV)

Conversations with Daddy
Day 10

Good Morning, Daughter
Day 11

I'm your creator, and I love you so very much. Pay attention to all types of my designs throughout the kingdom. They are things that I created. Just like you, they are specially designed. I know how you should work, and I know your capabilities. Prayerfully build a house of God designed to take authority in the kingdom of light.

Love,
Daddy

Remember that you molded me like clay.
Will you now turn me to dust again?
Did you not pour me out like milk and curdle me like cheese,
clothe me with skin and flesh
and knit me together with bones and sinews?
You gave me life and showed me kindness,
and in your providence watched over my spirit.

Job 10:9-12 (NIV)

Conversations with Daddy
Day 11

Good Morning, Daughter
Day 12

We are one, you and I. We are coupled together in my image. Don't ever doubt that I am with you. I am your Dad, gentle but firm, watching over you daily, like rushing running water. Take hold of me, Daughter, and stay with me. I will show you higher heights and deeper depths. Take hold of me, Daughter. I love you, and you can do this.

Love,
Daddy

The LORD will guide you continually,
giving you water when you are dry
and restoring your strength.
You will be like a well-watered garden,
like an ever-flowing spring.

Isaiah 58:11 (NLT)

Conversations with Daddy
Day 12

Good Morning, Daughter
Day 13

How beautiful this morning is! Walk with me, walk with me. We can walk through the day together. Exciting, isn't it? Walking with your Dad. Daughter, I have so many plans for you. You must walk them out with me. Plans to change the world and set the captives free. Plans to love folks, see them change. I chase after them. I love my people. I want to see them grow, live, and not die—to declare my works. Daughter, don't you see?

Love,
Dad

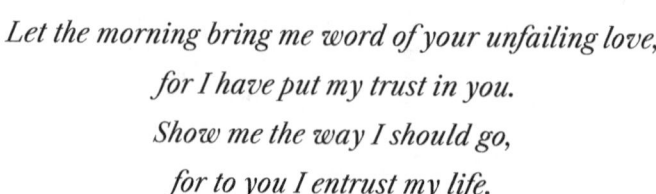

Let the morning bring me word of your unfailing love,
for I have put my trust in you.
Show me the way I should go,
for to you I entrust my life.

Psalm 143:8 (NIV)

Conversations with Daddy
Day 13

Good Morning, Daughter
Day 14

Today is an important day. I woke you up, and new mercies are available to you. Look for mercy like a lost puppy. Look and live. I love you, Daughter. You are special. I love you, Daughter. You are made in my image. Beautiful, free, gentle, and kind. I love you, Daughter.

He has shown you, O mortal, what is good.
And what does the Lord require of you?
To act justly and to love mercy
and to walk humbly with your God.

Micah 6:8 (NIV)

Conversations with Daddy
Day 14

Good Morning, Daughter
Day 15

The Earth is my place. I created it and placed you here. To love, to live, to grow, and to multiply for my glory. You are as lovely as anything, Daughter. Follow my ways so you can know me and follow me. I'm the key, and you're the door. Walk, live, learn, and love. You're my most precious gift, full of color and love.

I love you,
Dad

The earth is the Lord's and everything in it,
the world and all who live in it.

Psalm 24:1 (NIV)

Conversations with Daddy
Day 15

Good Morning, Daughter
Day 16

How are you this morning? This day marks the first day of many days. Watch, listen, and hear me. Watch, listen, and learn from me, Daughter. Spend time with me. Know me. I'm always here, watching you, guiding you, showing you things. You are my daughter, full of life. Follow me, Daughter, follow me.

Love,
Dad

Seek the Lord and his strength:
seek his presence continually!

Chronicles 16:11 (ESV)

Conversations with Daddy
Day 16

Good Morning, Daughter
Day 17

This is a beautiful day, full of adventures. Look for me today. Look and learn today. We are going to go through some things today. You and I. So watch and learn. Listen and I will tell you what to do. You and I. This is a beautiful day.

Love,
Dad

You keep him in perfect peace
whose mind is stayed on you.
Trust in the Lord forever,
for the Lord God is an everlasting rock.

Isaiah 26:3-4 (ESV)

Conversations with Daddy
Day 17

Good Morning, Daughter
Day 18

How lovely you are. I adorned you with my image. So lovely. Catch a glimpse of yourself, fearfully and wonderfully made. We have work to do. Keep calling those things that are not as though they are. Speak life and not death. Remember to keep your eye on me as you speak. Don't get distracted. Keep your eye on me and speak life.

Love,
Daddy

You are altogether beautiful, my darling;
there is no flaw in you.

Song of Solomon 4:7 (NIV)

Conversations with Daddy
Day 18

Good Morning, Daughter
Day 19

How excellent this morning is! We're going through this day in my grace. Soar through this day through my hand. Soar through this day in excellence. Soar, Daughter, fly by my grace, fly by my might. We are going to have a great day full of fun and joy. Laugh, Daughter, laugh. We are spending time together.

Love,
Daddy

All the days of the oppressed are wretched,
but the cheerful heart has a continual feast.

Proverbs 15:15 (NIV)

Conversations with Daddy
Day 19

Good Morning, Daughter
Day 20

How lovely this day is! Let's talk today, all day. Let's walk together and enjoy our day. You are my lovely creation. I have given you the keys to my kingdom. Where do you want to go? The sky's the limit. Use the tools I have given you and go.

Love,
Daddy

"I will give you the keys of the kingdom of heaven; whatever you bind on earth will be bound in heaven, and whatever you loose on earth will be loosed in heaven."

Matthew 16:19 (NIV)

Conversations with Daddy
Day 20

Good Morning, Daughter
Day 21

This is another morning I created, lovely in all its ways. Beautiful rays of the sun. I created those rays. And just as I created the sun's rays, I created you, Daughter, to extend your arms and shine like the morning sun. To have a full life and walk in confidence. I love you, Daughter, and we'll walk these days out together.

May the favor of the Lord our God rest on us;
establish the work of our hands for us—
yes, establish the work of our hands.

Psalm 90:17 (NIV)

Conversations with Daddy
Day 21

Good Morning, Daughter
Day 22

This is my day, and I am holy in all my ways. Because I am holy, you are too. Lift up your head and look, Daughter. Look at me and smile. I'm holding you. I'm holding you like I hold the stars in the night. I'm holding you like your mom used to hold you. I'm holding you because my love is infinite and vast. I'm holding you like the wind and the rain. I love you.

Speak to all the congregation of the people of Israel and say to them, You shall be holy, for I the Lord your God am holy.

Leviticus 19:2 (ESV)

Conversations with Daddy
Day 22

Good Morning, Daughter
Day 23

Today we will walk together. I understand what you're thinking and going through. But I'm your Father, and I love you forever. So don't look at the things around you. They are temporary. Look at me, and all will be well. I love you, and we are one.

*So we fix our eyes not on what is seen,
but on what is unseen,
since what is seen is temporary,
but what is unseen is eternal.*

2 Corinthians 4:18 (NIV)

Conversations with Daddy
Day 23

Good Morning, Daughter
Day 24

Hallowed be thy name. We are special, you and I. We are able to do exceedingly abundantly, you and I. Let us walk as Daddy and Daughter. You are my daughter and so special. I created all that you are. Every single hair on your head I created. Rejoice, Daughter, rejoice. I have all the answers. You only have to look and live.

Love,
Dad

At the end of that time, I, Nebuchadnezzar, raised my eyes toward heaven, and my sanity was restored. Then I praised the Most High; I honored and glorified him who lives forever.
His dominion is an eternal dominion;
his kingdom endures from generation to generation.

Daniel 4:34 (NIV)

Conversations with Daddy
Day 24

Good Morning, Daughter
Day 25

We are sitting here together, you and I, and we are enjoying the beginning of a new day. A new day with countless opportunities and bountiful abilities. Look around you, Daughter. Daddy owns it all, and if Daddy owns it all, so do you. Listen for me in every moment. Speak to me in all your ways. I'll respond, and you'll know it's me.

Teach me, Daddy, teach me to turn right or left.

I will teach you, Daughter, but you must listen.

Who among you will give ear to this,
will attend and listen for the time to come?

Isaiah 42:23 (RSV)

Conversations with Daddy
Day 25

Good Morning, Daughter
Day 26

Good morning, Daughter. It's been a while since you've picked up this pen to talk to me. I've been waiting to be able to say I love you in all my ways. Please don't forget to pause and see what I am going to say. This journey is ours, Daughter. I love you and adore being with you each and every day. Every moment we share is like a special time. Be still, Daughter. I have all situations under control. If you just bask in my glory, we will sail the horizons together. Be still, Daughter, and we'll sail together. I love you.

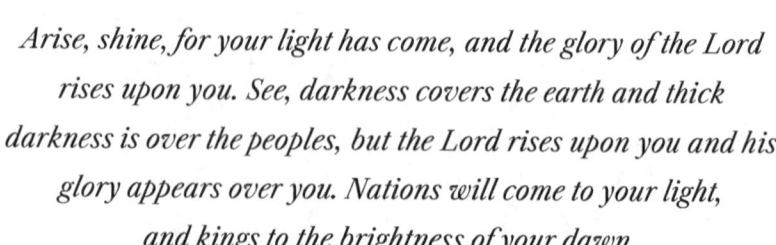

Arise, shine, for your light has come, and the glory of the Lord rises upon you. See, darkness covers the earth and thick darkness is over the peoples, but the Lord rises upon you and his glory appears over you. Nations will come to your light, and kings to the brightness of your dawn.

Isaiah 60:1-6 (NIV)

Conversations with Daddy
Day 26

Good Morning, Daughter
Day 27

Excellent day ahead. I'm making it that way. Have fun. Don't worry. I'm the king of everything. Remember that. I make everything good in its time. I'm the king, Daughter, and you are the princess.

Love,
Dad

I will exalt you, my God the king;
I will praise your name for ever and ever.

Psalm 145:1 (NIV)

Conversations with Daddy
Day 27

Good Morning, Daughter
Day 28

How beautiful is this day, another day I have given you. Rejoice, my Daughter, rejoice. Everything runs on my time. Rejoice, rejoice. I'm the Father, and you are the Daughter. Rejoice, rejoice. I have everything in the palm of my hand. Rejoice, rejoice. It's all okay, and I'm holding you up.

Sing aloud, O daughter of Zion;
shout, O Israel!
Rejoice and exult with all your heart,
O daughter of Jerusalem!
The Lord has taken away the judgments against you;
he has cleared away your enemies.

Zephaniah 3:14-17 (ESV)

Conversations with Daddy
Day 28

Good Morning, Daughter
Day 29

Hope is a special thing. Hope is what people live for in their day-to-day lives. I'm hope, and some people don't know me. Daughter, share what you know about me. I'm easy and my yoke is light. They need me for their lives, so share me, Daughter.

Love,
Dad

"For I know the plans I have for you," declares the Lord.
"Plans to prosper you and not to harm you.
Plans to give you hope and a future."

Jeremiah 29:11 (NIV)

Conversations with Daddy
Day 29

Good Morning, Daughter
Day 30

This is the day that I have made. It's my day. I am covering every nation and kingdom. It's my day, full of greatness. It's my day, full of joy. It's my day, gracious and magnificent. A day to be with me. To be with me, to love me, to see me, to hang out with me. I love you, Daughter. You're a part of me.

I will make you into a great nation,
and I will bless you;
I will make your name great,
and you will be a blessing.

Genesis 12:2 (NIV)

Conversations with Daddy
Day 30

Good Morning, Daughter
Day 31

Be still, Daughter. Be still. We are in another season. This is quite different from the last. I have your hand, and I'm leading you to victory. You will be victorious in me, and you will live and not die to declare the works of me, the Lord. I will show you how to be slow to speak and slow to anger. I have your hand, and I'm guiding you. Be still, Daughter, be still.

For the Lord your God is he that goes with you,
to fight for you against your enemies,
to give you the victory.

Psalm 145:1 (NIV)

Conversations with Daddy
Day 31

About the Author

Reverend Angela R. Carter is not your typical minister. A licensed cosmetologist with over thirty-five years of experience, she has owned and operated her own business, Angela's Ebony Hair Designs and Barbershop, for over twenty-seven years. Her entrepreneurial endeavors began in 1994 when she stepped out in faith, adhering to Matthew 19:26, "With God all things are possible." She has held fast to those principles ever since.

In addition to working in her business, she was led by the Lord to do ministry and outreach programs from her shop. Angela is the founder of the Women of Release Conference, designed to help women release the hurts of the past and embrace the powerful gifts God has placed inside of them for the future.

Angela was a member in the AME Church for over fifteen years and served as a local deacon and an ordained elder. She was the pastor of Beulah AME Church in Washington, Indiana, for five years.

Reverend Carter is currently ordained under the leadership of Pastor Johnnie Herald of Resurrection Life Ministries in Mitchell, Indiana. To God be the glory!

Contact Information

Angela R. Carter
1-812-327-0947

www.ingramcontent.com/pod-product-compliance
Lightning Source LLC
Chambersburg PA
CBHW050445010526
44118CB00013B/1695